The Tuning Fork

Lamar Coldwell

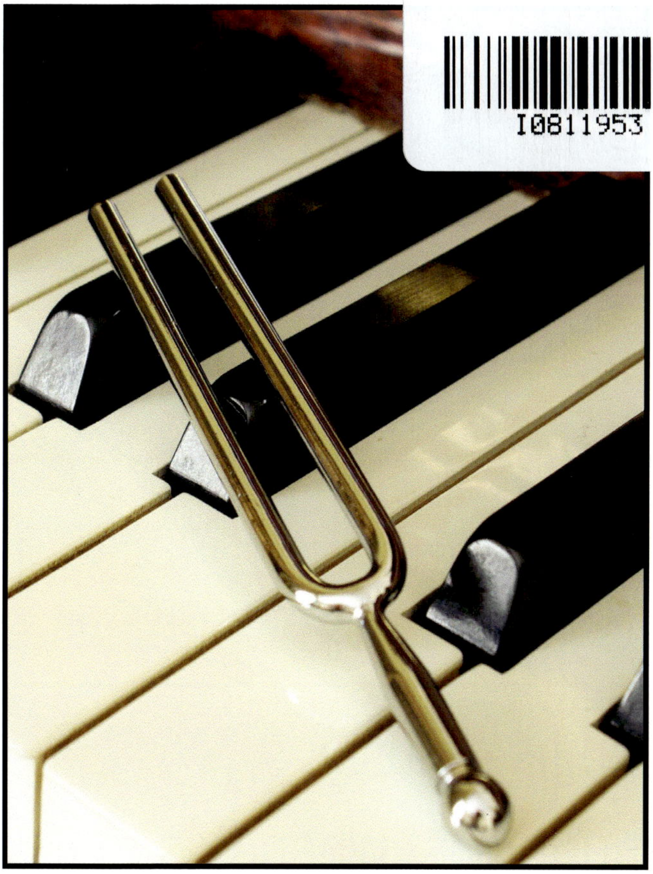

Rosen REAL READERS

Rosen Classroom™
New York

People like music.

It sounds best when it is in tune.

People tune instruments.
They use special tools.
They use a tuning fork.

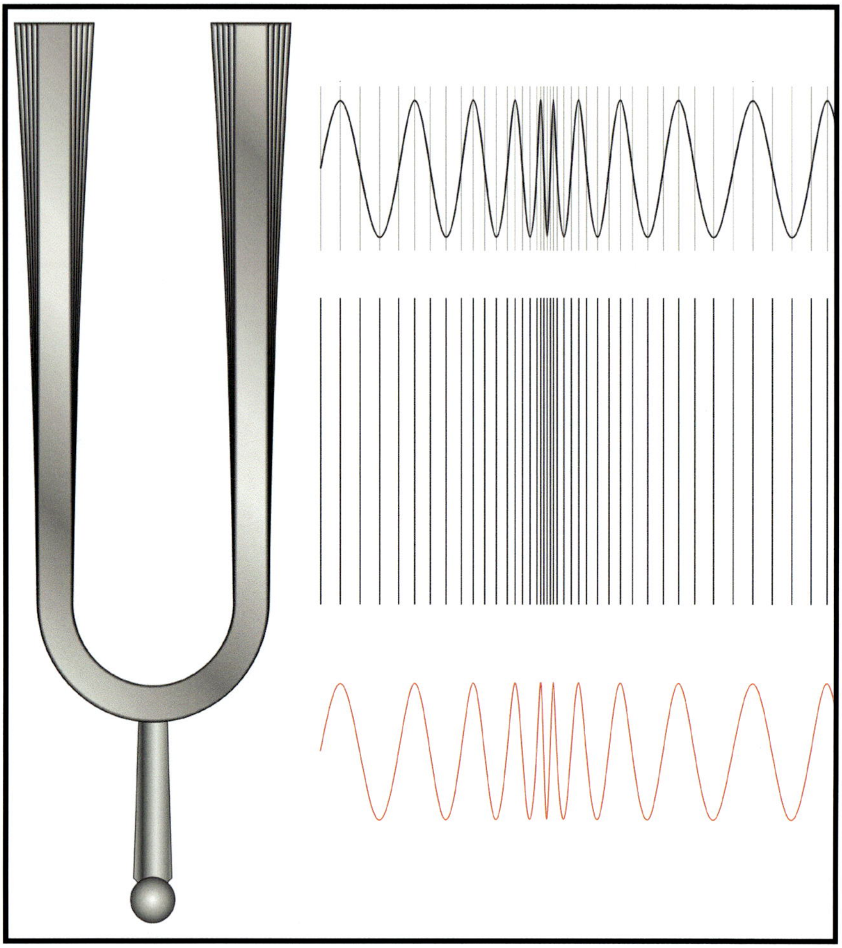

A tuning fork is hit.

It moves very fast.

It vibrates.

The vibration makes a sound.

The musician plays a note.
It makes the same sound as the tuning fork.
The guitar is in tune.

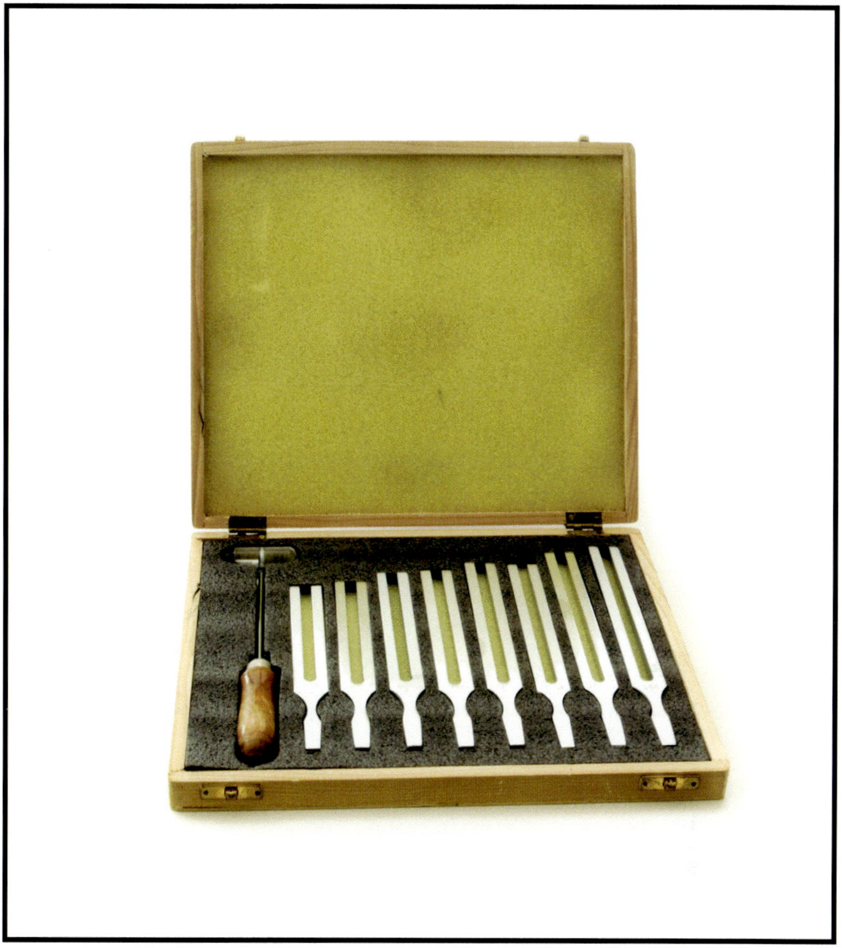

Tuning forks come in different sizes.

The size changes the sound.

Orchestras use tuning forks.
They help the music to be in tune.

Doctors use tuning forks.
They can help test hearing.

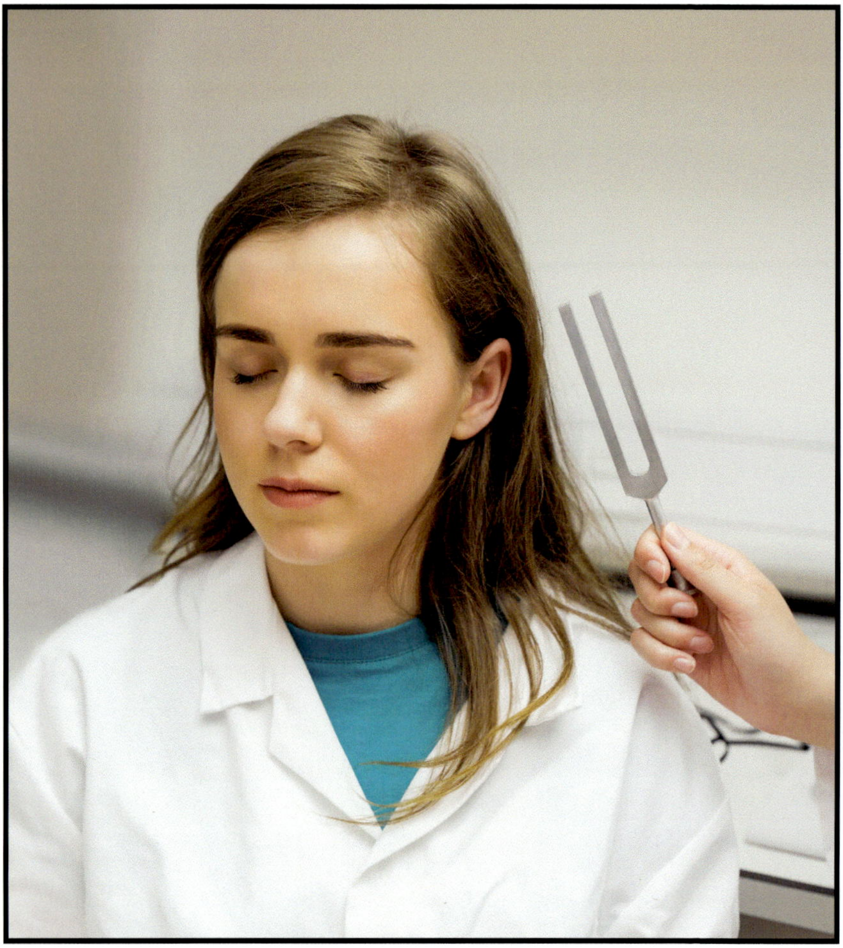

A doctor holds a tuning fork.
He holds it close to an ear.

A police officer checks car speeds.
First he makes sure his equipment works.
He uses a tuning fork.

Words to Know

doctor

instrument

orchestra

tuning fork